Magic
Sugar Cookie Dough
Recipes

How to Make
A Dozen Different Variations
From a Single Batch

Vicky Wells

Cover Artwork & Design by
Old Geezer Designs

Published in the United States by
Victoria House Bakery
an imprint of
DataIsland Software LLC,
Hollywood, Florida

ebooks.geezerguides.com

ISBN 978-0-9772346-2-2

Table of Contents

Introduction

Making these cookies with your kids is a great way for them to learn about baking along with simple, but important, rules for kitchen and food safely. They can learn how important it is to wash their hands before preparing any food (and several times during the preparation, too), how to handle raw eggs (don't eat raw cookie dough), how to safely use an oven without getting burned (oven mitts are important) and how to remove hot items from baking sheets (spatulas and cooking racks are good ideas).

This recipe was developed while making cookies with my kids when they were little. I hate to say it, but my grandchildren are now older than my kids were when I first developed this recipe.

We (my kids and I) all had different ideas about what kind of cookies we'd like to bake, so I decided to develop a recipe that could make several types of sugar cookies from a single batch.

It was a fun thing to do with my kids. They could each pick the type of cookie they wanted and then make and bake their own. They also had their own ideas about how the cookies themselves should look.

My eldest was very precise about his cookies. He was very good at making them all exactly the same size.

My middle child, the artist in the family, would hand-create each cookie in great detail. His cookies were truly works of art.

My baby was the absolute best at pressing the peanut butter cookies with fork tines to make a perfect pattern. She was also very good at making suggestions for different types of cookies.

This recipe makes about a dozen of each kind of cookie, if you choose to make four different kinds from a batch of basic dough. If you choose to make only one, two or three types of cookies from a single batch of basic dough, simply adjust the quantities accordingly.

The following basic recipe will allow you to create up to four different types of cookies, simply pick the ones you would like to make. The recipe doesn't work well if you try to create more than four different types as the dough will dry out much quicker if it is divided into amounts smaller than one-quarter of the basic recipes. Using one-quarter of the basic recipe for each type of cookies should net you approximately one dozen cookies. So, from a complete batch, you should end up with a total of four dozen cookies - a dozen of each kind you choose to make.

THE BASIC RECIPES

We'll start by making the basic recipe first. You can choose between either the plain sugar cookie dough recipe or the butterscotch sugar cookie dough recipe. Either basic dough will work with all of the add-ins but that's a matter of personal taste.

PLAIN SUGAR COOKIE DOUGH

INGREDIENTS

3½ - 4 Cups All Purpose Flour
1 Teaspoon Baking Powder
½ Teaspoon Salt
1 Cup Butter or Margarine
1½ Cups Sugar
2 Eggs
1½ Teaspoons Vanilla

DIRECTIONS

1. In a medium bowl, combine 3½ cups of flour, the baking powder and the salt. Mix thoroughly and set aside.

2. In a large bowl, cream the butter (or margarine) and gradually add the sugar, beating until the butter and sugar are well combined..

3. Add the eggs and blend thoroughly.

4. Add the vanilla and mix again.

5. Add the dry ingredients to the butter mixture gradually and mix after each addition. I like to do the final mixing with my hands. If you find that the dough is sticking to your hands you can add up to another 1/2 cup of flour. Be sure to add it gradually so that you don't end up with a dough that is too dry.

6. When the desired consistency has been achieved, divide the dough into four equal pieces (if you plan to make four different types of cookies). I weighed the dough to make it easier to divide. I found this recipe made about 40 ounces of dough, so I divided it into four 10-ounce pieces.

7. Once you have incorporated the add-ins into the dough, wrap the pieces tightly in plastic wrap and chill for one hour. Chilling the dough will make it easier to work with and less sticky.

Note: The Rolled Sugar Cookies don't have any add-ins, but you should still chill the dough for an hour before rolling it out.

Butterscotch Sugar Cookie Dough

Ingredients

3½ - 4 Cups All Purpose Flour
1 Teaspoon Baking Powder
½ Teaspoon Salt
1 Cup Butter or Margarine
1½ Cups Firmly Packed Brown Sugar
2 Eggs
1½ Teaspoons Vanilla

Directions

1. In a medium bowl, combine 3½ cups of flour, the baking powder and the salt. Mix thoroughly and set aside.

2. In a large bowl, cream the butter (or margarine) and gradually add the sugar, beating until the butter and sugar are well combined..

3. Add the eggs and blend thoroughly.

4. Add the vanilla and mix again.

5. Add the dry ingredients to the butter mixture gradually and mix after each addition. I like to do the final mixing with my hands. If you find that the dough is sticking to your hands you can add up to another 1/2 cup of flour. Be sure to add it gradually so that you don't end up with a dough that is too dry.

6. When the desired consistency has been achieved, divide the dough into four equal pieces (if you plan to make four different types of cookies). I weighed the dough to make it easier to divide. I found this recipe made about 40 ounces of dough, so I divided it into four 10-ounce pieces.

7. Once you have incorporated the add-ins into the dough, wrap the pieces tightly in plastic wrap and chill for one hour. Chilling the dough will make it easier to work with and less sticky.

Note: The Rolled Sugar Cookies don't have any add-ins, but you should still chill the dough for an hour before rolling it out.

Cookie Variations Using the Basic dough

Now it's time to explore all of the variations we can make using the basic Sugar Cookie dough - either plain or butterscotch.

This sugar cookie dough can be either rolled or formed to make the various cookies and following are instructions for both types.

ROLLED SUGAR COOKIE VARIATIONS

A lot of the time sugar cookies are rolled, making them thin and crispy. The following variations are those types of cookies.

As these cookies require no add-ins, you can use all, or a portion of the basic dough recipe - plain or butterscotch - to make as many cookies as you'd like. However, for the instructions, we'll assume that you are using one-quarter of the basic dough.

Plain Rolled Sugar Cookies

Directions

1. Lightly flour a flat surface where you can roll out the dough.
2. Using one-quarter of the chilled Basic Sugar Cookie Dough, take a portion of the chilled dough and form it into a thick disc.
3. Place it on the floured surface and sprinkle a bit more flour on the top.
4. Roll out the dough as thin as possible.
5. Use a cookie cutter to cut out whatever shapes you would like to make.

   Note: You can re-use any of the dough left over after cutting out the shapes by balling it back up again and then rolling it out. But, only do this once, as it will get much to dry after that.

6. Carefully transfer the sugar cookies to the greased cookie sheet.
7. Sprinkle sugar on the top of each cookie. You can use colored sugar if you like.
8. Bake at 375°F for about 6 to 8 minutes. Watch them carefully as they can brown very quickly.
9. Carefully transfer the cookies to a cooling rack and allow to cool completely.

Sandwich Sugar Cookies

Directions

1. Lightly flour a flat surface where you can roll out the dough.
2. Using one-quarter of the chilled Basic Sugar Cookie Dough, take a portion of the chilled dough and form it into a thick disc.
3. Place it on the floured surface and sprinkle a bit more flour on the top.
4. Roll out as thin as possible.
5. Use a cookie cutter to cut out circles to be used for the bottom of the sandwich. For the tops, use the same size cookie cutter and use a much smaller one to create the hole in the center.

   Note: You can re-use any of the dough left over after cutting out the shapes by balling it back up again and then rolling it out. But, only do this once, as it will get much to dry after that.

6. Carefully transfer the sugar cookies to the greased cookie sheet.
7. Sprinkle sugar on the "top" cookies only.
8. Bake at 375°F for about 6 to 8 minutes. Watch them carefully as they can brown very quickly.
9. Transfer to a cooling rack and allow to cool completely.
10. Once the cookies are cooled, spread a thin layer of jam on the bottom cookie and place a top cookie on the top the make the sandwich.

Turnover Sugar Cookies

Directions

1. Lightly flour a flat surface where you can roll out the dough.
2. Using one-quarter of the chilled Basic Sugar Cookie Dough, take a portion of the chilled dough and form it into a thick disc.
3. Place it on the floured surface and sprinkle a bit more flour on the top.
4. Roll out as thin as possible.
5. Use a 4-inch round cookie cutter to cut out circles.
6. Place a small spoonful of apple butter, or your choice of jam, on each circle and gently fold in half, pressing the edges together with the tines of a fork.
7. Carefully transfer the turnover cookies to the greased cookie sheet.
8. Bake at 375°F for about 8 to 10 minutes or until nicely browned.
9. Transfer to a cooling rack and allow to cool completely.

FORMED SUGAR COOKIES

Formed sugar cookies are generally chewier than the rolled type and lend themselves better to all kinds of add-ins.

Following are several ideas for tasty and interesting sugar cookies.

CANDY CANE COOKIES

INGREDIENTS

¼ of the Basic Sugar Cookie Dough
¼ Cup of crushed candy canes

DIRECTIONS

1. Knead the crushed candy canes into the dough making sure they are well mixed. Refrigerate, well wrapped in plastic wrap, for one hour.

2. Preheat the oven to 375°F and grease the cookie sheet.

3. Form the chilled dough into 12 small balls by rolling between the palms of your hands.

4. Place each ball onto the greased cookie sheet and press down with the flat of your fingers.

5. Bake at 375°F for about 10 to 12 minutes. The bottoms will be brown and edges will just be starting to brown.

6. Gently transfer to a wire rack and allow to cool completely.

Chocolate Chip Cookies

Ingredients

¼ of the Basic Sugar Cookie Dough
¼ Cup chocolate chips

Directions

1. Knead the chocolate chips into the dough making sure they are well mixed. Refrigerate, well wrapped in plastic wrap, for one hour.
2. Preheat the oven to 375°F and grease the cookie sheet.
3. Form the chilled dough into 12 small balls by rolling between the palms of your hands.
4. Place each ball onto the greased cookie sheet and press down with the flat of your fingers.
5. Bake at 375°F for about 10 to 12 minutes. The bottoms will be brown and edges will just be starting to brown.
6. Gently transfer to a wire rack and allow to cool completely.

CHOCOLATE MINT COOKIES

INGREDIENTS

¼ of the Basic Sugar Cookie Dough
¼ cup of chocolate mint chips, or chopped chocolate peppermint
patties

DIRECTIONS

1. Knead the chocolate mint chips (or chopped chocolate peppermint patties) into the dough making sure they are well mixed. Refrigerate, well wrapped in plastic wrap, for one hour.
2. Preheat the oven to 375°F and grease the cookie sheet.
3. Form the chilled dough into 12 small balls by rolling between the palms of your hands.
4. Place each ball onto the greased cookie sheet and press down with the flat of your fingers.
5. Bake at 375°F for about 10 to 12 minutes. The bottoms will be brown and edges will just be starting to brown.
6. Gently transfer to a wire rack and allow to cool completely.

Coconut Cookies

Ingredients

¼ of the Basic Sugar Cookie Dough
½ cup shredded coconut

Directions

1. Knead the shredded coconut into the dough making sure they are well mixed. Refrigerate, well wrapped in plastic wrap, for one hour.
2. Preheat the oven to 375°F and grease the cookie sheet.
3. Form the chilled dough into 12 small balls by rolling between the palms of your hands.
4. Place each ball onto the greased cookie sheet and press down with the flat of your fingers.
5. Bake at 375°F for about 10 to 12 minutes. The bottoms will be brown and edges will just be starting to brown.
6. Gently transfer to a wire rack and allow to cool completely.

Date & Nut Cookies

Ingredients

¼ of the Basic Sugar Cookie Dough
a total of ⅓ cup of chopped dates and nuts

Directions

1. Knead the chopped dates and nuts into the dough making sure they are well mixed. Refrigerate, well wrapped in plastic wrap, for one hour.
2. Preheat the oven to 375°F and grease the cookie sheet.
3. Form the chilled dough into 12 small balls by rolling between the palms of your hands.
4. Place each ball onto the greased cookie sheet and press down with the flat of your fingers.
5. Bake at 375°F for about 10 to 12 minutes. The bottoms will be brown and edges will just be starting to brown.
6. Gently transfer to a wire rack and allow to cool completely.

M&Ms Cookies

Ingredients

¼ of the Basic Sugar Cookie Dough
¼ cup of chopped M&Ms candies of your choice (or any other type of candy coated chocolate pieces)

Directions

1. Knead the chopped candies into the dough making sure they are well mixed. Refrigerate, well wrapped in plastic wrap, for one hour.
2. Preheat the oven to 375°F and grease the cookie sheet.
3. Form the chilled dough into 12 small balls by rolling between the palms of your hands.
4. Place each ball onto the greased cookie sheet and press down with the flat of your fingers.
5. Bake at 375°F for about 10 to 12 minutes. The bottoms will be brown and edges will just be starting to brown.
6. Gently transfer to a wire rack and allow to cool completely.

Nut Cookies

Ingredients

¼ of the Basic Sugar Cookie Dough
¼ cup of chopped nuts of your choice

Directions

1. Knead the chopped nuts into the dough making sure they are well mixed. Refrigerate, well wrapped in plastic wrap, for one hour.
2. Preheat the oven to 375°F and grease the cookie sheet.
3. Form the chilled dough into 12 small balls by rolling between the palms of your hands.
4. Place each ball onto the greased cookie sheet and press down with the flat of your fingers.
5. Bake at 375°F for about 10 to 12 minutes. The bottoms will be brown and edges will just be starting to brown.
6. Gently transfer to a wire rack and allow to cool completely.

Peanut Butter Cookies

Ingredients

¼ of the Basic Sugar Cookie Dough
⅓ Cup of peanut butter - plain or chunky

Directions

1. Knead the peanut butter into the dough making sure they are well mixed. Refrigerate, well wrapped in plastic wrap, for one hour.

2. Preheat the oven to 375°F and grease the cookie sheet.

3. Form the chilled dough into 12 small balls by rolling between the palms of your hands.

4. Place each ball onto the greased cookie sheet and press down with the flat of your fingers, then use fork tines to make lines first one way and then at 90 degrees.

5. Bake at 375°F for about 10 to 12 minutes. The bottoms will be brown and edges will just be starting to brown.

6. Gently transfer to a wire rack and allow to cool completely.

PECAN SANDIES

INGREDIENTS

¼ of the Basic Sugar Cookie Dough

¼ Cup pecans, chopped to the consistency of a coarse meal

DIRECTIONS

1. Knead the chopped pecans into the dough making sure they are well mixed. Refrigerate, well wrapped in plastic wrap, for one hour.
2. Preheat the oven to 375°F and grease the cookie sheet.
3. Form the chilled dough into 12 small balls by rolling between the palms of your hands.
4. Place each ball onto the greased cookie sheet and press down with the flat of your fingers.
5. Bake at 375°F for about 10 to 12 minutes. The bottoms will be brown and edges will just be starting to brown.
6. Gently transfer to a wire rack and allow to cool completely.

RAISIN COOKIES

INGREDIENTS

¼ of the Basic Sugar Cookie Dough

¼ Cup raisins

DIRECTIONS

1. Knead the raisins into the dough making sure they are well mixed. Refrigerate, well wrapped in plastic wrap, for one hour.
2. Preheat the oven to 375°F and grease the cookie sheet.
3. Form the chilled dough into 12 small balls by rolling between the palms of your hands.
4. Place each ball onto the greased cookie sheet and press down with the flat of your fingers.
5. Bake at 375°F for about 10 to 12 minutes. The bottoms will be brown and edges will just be starting to brown.
6. Gently transfer to a wire rack and allow to cool completely.

Rum Raisin Cookies

Note 1: You'll need to plan ahead for these cookies as the raisins need to be soaked for a couple of hours.

Note 2: When using the Butterscotch Basic Sugar Cookie Dough with this recipe you get Butter Rum Raisin Cookies.

Ingredients

2 Tablespoons rum or rum flavoring
¼ Cup raisins
¼ of the Basic Sugar Cookie Dough

Directions

1. Soak the raisins in rum (or rum flavoring) for two hours and then drain and pat dry

2. Knead the raisins into the dough making sure they are well mixed. Refrigerate, well wrapped in plastic wrap, for one hour.

3. Preheat the oven to 375°F and grease the cookie sheet.

4. Form the chilled dough into 12 small balls by rolling between the palms of your hands.

5. Place each ball onto the greased cookie sheet and press down with the flat of your fingers.

6. Bake at 375°F for about 10 to 12 minutes. The bottoms will be brown and edges will just be starting to brown.

7. Gently transfer to a wire rack and allow to cool completely.

SESAME COOKIES

INGREDIENTS

¼ of the Basic Sugar Cookie Dough
2-3 Tablespoons sesame seeds

DIRECTIONS

1. Preheat the oven to 375°F and grease the cookie sheet.
2. Form the chilled basic dough into 12 small balls by rolling between the palms of your hands. Dip the top of each ball into the sesame seeds.
3. Place each ball onto the greased cookie sheet, sesame seed side up, and press down with the flat of your fingers.
4. Bake at 375°F for about 10 to 12 minutes. The bottoms will be brown and edges will just be starting to brown.
5. Gently transfer to a wire rack and allow to cool completely.

And, last but not least ...

Imagination Cookies

Simply use your imagination to make cookie variations. Please feel free to let us know the versions you have come up with and we may include them in an update, giving you credit for the creation.

Free Gift Now
+ Get Free Books Later

As a special thank you for purchasing this book we want to give you a free gift. Just visit this secret web page and pick up your free copy of "Our Favorite Detox and Weight Loss Slow Cooker Recipes"

http://ebooks.geezerguides.com/your-free-gift/

Also, each time any of our current or new books are offered for free, we'll be sure to tell you and hope you would take the time to review some of them.

One of the toughest things for an independent author is to get honest reviews for their books. We will gladly notify you of the availability of free copies of our books in hopes that, if you like them, you will post an honest review.

There's no catch and no obligation, just check the box on our website. Thank you. (We promise - NO SPAM - we hate it too)

Please Review Magic Sugar Cookie Dough Recipes

Now that you've reached the end of the this book, we would really appreciate you taking a moment to post a review on your local Amazon site: Just use the URL below to reach this book's page on Amazon.

http://geni.us/Cookie

ABOUT THE AUTHOR

Vicky Wells is a real person who has a real life. She is a retired customer service consultant who spends summers in Northern Canada and winters in the Bahamas.

She and her husband Geoff write books on many subjects under various pen names. Mostly healthy living and cookbooks but also children's books, science fiction and anti-establishment rants.

If you want to know more please visit http://geoffandvickywells.com

The site is often out of date, incomplete and not particularly interesting but you are welcome to check it out. Much the same can be said for the blog at http://geezerguides.com

The most interesting site is at http://terranovian.com but if you visit be warned that you may be turned into a raving activist and get banned from all your friends cocktail parties.

She also has an author page on Amazon

http://amazon.com/author/vickyjwells

Contact Us

Life keeps us quite busy but we try to keep up with posts on several social networks and we welcome you to join us. If you visit please "Like" the page.

Facebook

https://www.facebook.com/pages/The-Terra-Novian-Way/179965592154046

https://www.facebook.com/GeezerGuides

https://www.facebook.com/ReluctantVegetarians

Twitter

http://twitter.com/TerraNovianWay

http://twitter.com/GeezerGuides

https://twitter.com/NutritiousFood

Goodreads

https://www.goodreads.com/author/show/2864210.Vicky_Wells

Shelfari

http://www.shelfari.com/authors/a1002691403/Geoff-Wells/

Google+

https://plus.google.com/104962434482327095816/posts

YouTube

https://www.youtube.com/channel/UCw-aid2E0NB8nUcLjUfiYeA

More books from Geezer Guide Publishing

The companion book to this one is "How To Make Perfect Pastry - Every Time". If you want to know how to make the best tasting pastry you have ever had, this is the book for you.

Made in the USA
Monee, IL
07 July 2026

56551548R00017